WORLD SERIES CHAMPIONS
BOSTON RED SOX

AARON FRISCH

CREATIVE EDUCATION

The Red Sox are a team in **Major League Baseball**. They play in Boston, Massachusetts. Boston is one of the oldest cities in America. The first school in America was built there.

The Red Sox have a stadium called Fenway Park. Their uniforms are red, blue, and white. The Red Sox play lots of games against teams called the Blue Jays, Orioles, Rays, and Yankees. The Red Sox and Yankees are **rivals**.

Fenway Park

CY YOUNG

OUTFIELDER
TRIS SPEAKER

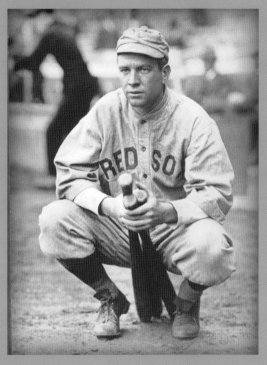

Boston started playing in 1901. The team had a great pitcher named Cy Young. In 1903, he helped Boston win the first World Series ever played!

Pitcher Bill Dineen

The Red Sox got a pitcher named Babe Ruth after that. Ruth was very strong. He hit 714 home runs in his **career**! He helped the Red Sox win four more World Series.

BABE RUTH

OUTFIELDER
TED WILLIAMS

SECOND BASEMAN
BOBBY DOERR

In 1920, Babe Ruth left Boston.
The Red Sox became a bad team
until outfielder Ted Williams came
to Boston. He helped the Red Sox
get to the World Series in 1946.
But they lost.

CARL YASTRZEMSKI

Outfielder Carl Yastrzemski (*yuh-STREM-skee*) helped Boston win lots of games after that. But the Red Sox finished in second place a lot behind the Yankees. The Red Sox got to the World Series in 1967 and 1975. But they lost both times.

PITCHER
ROGER CLEMENS

OUTFIELDER
DWIGHT EVANS

The Red Sox added pitcher Roger Clemens in 1984. They almost won the World Series in 1986. But they lost the last two games.

17

PITCHER
PEDRO MARTINEZ

In 2004, the Red Sox played the Yankees in the **playoffs**. The Yankees won the first three games. But first baseman David Ortiz helped the Red Sox win four games in a row! Then the Red Sox won the World Series. It was their first world championship in 86 years! In 2007, they won the World Series again.

FIRST BASEMAN
DAVID ORTIZ

21

OUTFIELDER

MANNY RAMIREZ

22

WORLD SERIES CHAMPIONS
BOSTON RED SOX

Pitcher Jonathan Papelbon

Jonathan Papelbon was another good Red Sox player. He was a pitcher who could throw the ball hard. Boston fans hope that today's Red Sox will win the World Series again soon!

GLOSSARY

career — all of the seasons that a player plays

Major League Baseball — a group of 30 baseball teams that play against each other; major-league teams have the best players in the world

playoffs — games that are played after the season to see which team is the champion

rivals — teams that play extra hard against each other

RED SOX FACTS

Team colors: red, blue, and white

First home stadium: Huntington Avenue Grounds

Home stadium today: Fenway Park

League/Division: American League, Eastern Division

First season: 1901

World Series championships: 1903, 1912, 1915, 1916, 1918, 2004, 2007

Team name: The Red Sox got their name because their uniforms had red socks. Red Sox became the team name in 1908. Before that, people called them different names like the Pilgrims, Puritans, and Americans.

Major League Baseball Web site for kids:
http://www.mlb.com/mlb/kids/

INDEX

WORLD SERIES CHAMPIONS

BOSTON RED SOX

Published by Creative Education
P.O. Box 227, Mankato, Minnesota 56002
Creative Education is an imprint of The Creative Company
www.thecreativecompany.us

Design and production by Blue Design
Printed in the United States of America

Photographs by Corbis (Bettmann, Amanda Hall/Robert Harding World Imagery, JESSICA
RINALDI/Reuters), Getty Images (APA, Al Bello, Bruce Bennett Studios, Otto Greule Jr/
Allsport, Andy Hayt, Hulton Archive, Carl Iwasaki//Time Life Pictures, Brad Mangin/MLB
Photos, National Baseball Hall of Fame Library/MLB Photos, Gary Newkirk, Art Rickerby//
Time Life Pictures, Photo File, Rich Pilling/MLB Photos, Herb Scharfman/Sports Imagery, Joseph
Scherschel//Time Life Pictures, Ezra Shaw, Rick Stewart, Ron Vesely/MLB Photos)

Library of Congress Cataloging-in-Publication Data

Frisch, Aaron.
Boston Red Sox / by Aaron Frisch.
p. cm. — (World Series champions)
Includes index.
ISBN 978-1-58341-694-5
1. Boston Red Sox (Baseball team)—History—Juvenile literature. I. Title. II. Series.

GV875.B62F73 2009
796.357'640974461—dc22   2008003765

First edition
9 8 7 6 5 4 3 2 1

Cover: First baseman David Ortiz (top), pitcher Joe Wood (bottom)
Page 1: Third baseman Wade Boggs
Page 3: Shortstop Nomar Garciaparra